Monsters

Short Monologues from the Dark Side

By
Chris Bullard

Blue Moon Plays

Monster: Short Monologues from the Dark Side
CAUTION: Professionals and amateurs are hereby warned that performance of TITLE is subject to payment of a royalty unless written permission is given waiving such fee. The Play is fully protected under the copyright laws of the United States of America, and of all countries covered by the International Copyright Union (including the Dominion of Canada and the rest of the British Commonwealth), and of all countries covered by the Pan-American Copyright Convention, the Universal Copyright Convention, and the Berne Convention, and of all countries with which the United States has reciprocal copyright relations. All rights, including professional/amateur stage rights, motion picture, recitation, lecturing, public reading, radio broadcasting, television, video or sound recording, all other forms of mechanical or electronic reproduction, such as CD-ROM, CD-I, DVD, information storage and retrieval systems and photo-copying, and the rights of translation into foreign languages, are strictly reserved. Particular emphasis is placed upon the matter of readings, permission for which must be secured from the Author in writing.

Anyone receiving permission to produce the Play is required to give credit to the Author as sole and exclusive Author of the Play on the title page of all programs distributed in connection with performances of the Play and in all instances in which the title of the Play appears for purposes of advertising, publicizing or otherwise exploiting the Play and/or a production thereof. Author's name must be one-third the size of the title.

All performances and or readings of this script, whether or not admission fees are required, must apply for and receive a Performance License.

ISBN: 978-1-943416-61-5
Printed in the USA
Published by Blue Moon Plays
1385 Fordham Road, Ste 105-279
Virginia Beach, VA 23464

Monsters:
Short Monologues from the Dark Side

This script can be performed by community, educational, or professional theaters either for the stage, the classroom, or as reader's theater.

Copyright law prevents this script from being copied or shared by any technical or digital means.

If you wish to perform these scripts, you must do the following:

1. Purchase sufficient scripts for your performance :
   - Purchase a Multicopy PDF which allows you to print sufficient copies of this script (one for each cast member, plus 4 for the crew) at Blue Moon Plays. Click Return to Merchant to download your printable PDF. A link to the download will also be emailed to you, along with a link to the application for performance license.

   OR

   - Purchase sufficient printed hard copies (one for each cast member, plus 4 for the crew) - an automatic 10 percent discount is applied to multiple printed hardcopies at the point of ordering.
2. Apply for a performance license.
3. Pay a Performance Fee for the specific days of your performances.

All scripts and licenses shall be obtained at Blue Moon Plays at www.havescripts.com

If you wish to make changes in the script of any kind, you must receive permission from the publisher or the playwright. Permission is usually granted readily when schools or theaters face casting problems and the changes do not affect the quality or intent of the original.

For information, visit www.havescripts.com
email info@bluemoonplays.com or call 757-816-1164

Monster

Igor must have lifted a brain from a loser.
The one he gave me doesn't like being stuck in this retread corpse.
Whine, whine: the rusty bolts, the mismatched parts.

My head hurts just thinking about it.
So I don't.

But my body is sick because I pay attention to my brain.
It feels restrained by that grey slug up in my skull.
No wonder I can't find a mate.

Their bickering gets me into so much trouble,
I try to pretend I don't really exist.

I can't favor one over the other.
It's like your parents asking you which one of them you want to live
with.
I'd have to lose them both to start being normal.

If we all worked together I know we could be some sort of heroic ideal.
Instead, it's just one social disaster after another.

I said something stupid to that girl at the pond.
I gobbled down that blind guy's soup.
My best friend didn't even want me at his wedding.

Monsters are built from human parts.
How I am is how I was made.

When the villagers show up with torches I try to blend in,
but all I can do is mumble, "Smash, kill, destroy."

I'd probably be better off alone.
Out on the ice, for example, I could contemplate the sublime.
Maybe, I should give up on my dream of living in a castle.

I'd like to undo the threads holding me together.
I'd like to find some part of me that could live outside of me

as an object, red and bleeding and representing my true self.
        --first published in *The Atlanta Review*

v

Table of Contents

SLEEPING BEAUTY

Interior. A motel somewhere. JOHN, a middle aged man, dressed in a flannel shirt, jeans and work boots, sits at a table. He has a bottle of Jack Daniels and a paper cup in front of him.

JOHN
After my wife, Shirley, died. And it took a year of pain and misery. Lord, that woman suffered. She had stomach cancer and even the pills didn't help. I never saw anyone in such pain.

(Pause)
Anyway, after my wife died, my daughter, Becky cried every night for her. She was only twelve that year and her mother had been everything to her. Me, I was around, but I was never a daddy that Oprah would have approved of, or Dr. Phil.

(Pours himself a shot and takes a drink)
I loved her though. Anyway, I had been getting disability for a few years. It wasn't a lot of money, but it helped with the bills and when Shirley was working we made out all right. I guess you could say I had my own issues. I kept to myself. I didn't like being around other people. Maybe, that's what I thought. That Becky was like other people.

(Pause)
So, it took me a while to respond. To realize what my wife's death had done to Becky. How she needed someone.

(Pause)
One night she came to me while I was lying on the sofa, watching TV. I always had the TV on, but I never really paid attention. I guess I was just lost in my own dreams. Anyway, she was bawling her poor little heart out. And she lay down beside me while her hot little tears fell on my undershirt. I mean, I could feel my shirt really getting soaked. And I hugged her and

1

tried real hard to think of what I could do to make her feel better. What I could do to ease the pain, so to speak.

(*Pause*)
And then I remembered some of the stories that my Mom had told me. Bedtime stories, but the real old ones. Fairy tales. Mom knew I loved those stories. Sometimes my brothers would push me around and I'd get real sad.. I was the littlest one. So, when I got real sad, she would tell me one of those stories. And one of my favorites was about Lazy Jack and how he done all these foolish things and how he'd been so ridiculous that he'd made the princess smile. The princess who would never smile. So, I told Becky that story and she listened and then, God dammit, I could see a little smile on her face. Then, I tickled her and she said stop, but I knew she didn't want me to, so I kept making her laugh. We had a good time for a while. Finally, I let her go to sleep right there beside me. And I thought, maybe, for a minute or two, she's forgotten about her mother and the suffering we've all gone through.

(*Pours himself a shot and takes a drink*)
She loved those stories. Hell, we both did. It was the fantasy that drew you in and made you forget everything else. I mean, there was always some task that the king would set a boy to. If you do this, you'll win my daughter's hand and the keys to the kingdom. I guess it was sort of the lottery of olden days. And the girls were always venturing out and dealing with wolves and beasts, but never getting scared. They knew the beast would always turn out to be good and kind.   I would take Becky to the library and we'd check out something by Hans Christian Anderson, or the Grimm brothers. And, every night I'd read to her until she went to sleep.

(*Pause*)
Maybe, I got too indulgent with her, but it made her so happy. I ordered her one of those princess costumes from a catalogue. They have them for Halloween. Becky would put it on every

night when I'd read her a story. And, okay, this really sounds crazy, but I got some cinder blocks from a construction site and I stacked them up in the cellar, and they made a wall that really looked like it was part of a castle. So, I would come down the stairs and Becky would be on the other side of the basement behind the cinder blocks and she would call out to me, "What is your quest, good sir?" and I would call back, "To read the Princess a bedtime story, of course." Then, she'd say "Enter" and, one night, finally, lowered the drawbridge for me.

(*Pause*)
Sometimes, I'd read a story and we'd make a game of it. I'd read about the boy who found a dish with a white snake on it and when he nibbled on the snake, he could understand what the animals were saying. Or, how the Princess poured a bucket of fish over the boy who didn't know fear and how that taught him to shudder. We had such good times. I mean, sure it would have been better if Becky could have found some friends, but we were living on the edge of Camden, in one of those neighborhoods that had changed real quick. All the girls her age were already shooting up and joining gangs, for God's sake. And the boys! I hated that she had to go to school with them.

(*Pours a shot and takes a drink*)
This went on for about a year and then I ran into the wicked witch. She wasn't the Disney wicked witch, of course. She didn't have a big bucket, or a pointed hat. She was sorta squat with big glasses and curly hair and she wore a business suit. But she was the wicked witch, alright. She was some sort of assistant principal at Becky's school. She phoned me one day and said I had to come in for a conference. I asked Becky what was going on, but she just shrugged and said "I don't know" in that sweet little innocent voice.

(*Puts glass on table, moves it in a circle while talks*)
So I went. That's when the wicked witch unloaded all this crap about Becky and how she was saying inappropriate things to the

boys and how she had inappropriate physical contact with one kid and how she wasn't acting appropriately for her age. Appropriate was a big word for the wicked witch. It worked like a spell for her. She could make fathers disappear with that one.

(*Pause*)
So she asked me about this and she asked me about that and we went round and round the bush, but I couldn't convince her that everything was on the up and up, that Becky had just picked up some stupid stuff around the school, which was a pretty rough place, if you know what I mean. Instead, the wicked witch told me there was gonna be some sort of God damn review and that there would be counselors and social workers and all the king's men there and they would have a few questions about me and Becky. I wanted to start a big bonfire for the witch, but I only said "good day" and went home to wait for Becky.

(*Pours and drinks, pours and drinks again*)
They were going to take Annabelle Lee away from her kingdom by the sea.

(*Pause*)
I knew it. They knew it. I don't know if Becky knew it. I don't know what she would have said about us and our games and our stories. Nobody would have understood.

(*Pause*)
That night, I made her favorite, macaroni and cheese, and I served her a big glass of sparkling apple cider. She thought it was like having champagne. After dinner, I read her Sleeping Beauty. "What do you think it's like to sleep for a hundred years?" I asked her, but she was already asleep.

(*Pause*)
The pills that the doctors had prescribed for her mother were pretty strong. I figured that I had put enough of them in her

apple cider. "A hundred years. That's all it takes until Prince Charming comes. " I said.

(*Pause, caps bottle*)
I had already taken the top off her toy chest and moved it down to the cellar. I took Becky and laid her in the toy chest. We had this glass table top that her mother had bought from Pier One and I put it on the top of the chest. It was like The Glass Coffin. You could see how peaceful she was there. Then, I left.

(*Pause, wads up cup*)
So, call me a knight errant, or a boy with no fortune, or God damn Puss-in-Boats, but I'm off to see the world and do great deeds. Maybe, it'll all be over real fast, but, maybe, I'll keep going for a hundred years and, one day, the stag will call to me, or the fairy will give me a glass key, and I'll find her again and take her out of the coffin where she's been sleeping and give her a kiss. And someone will say, "And they lived happily afterwards." And then they'll say, "The end." And it'll be the best story ever.

DRIVER

The stage is dark except for a light above MARIANNE, a woman in her 70s. MARIANNE wears a flowered dress and has a yellow silk scarf around her throat. She wears a bandage around her head. MARIANNE is seated on a green couch. There is a bowl of asters and wild flowers on a table in front of the couch. She has her purse next to her on the couch.

MARIANNE

I really don't know what has happened to make people so rude. They bowl you over in stores. They push past you on the sidewalk. They honk at you on the roads.

(Pause)
Just the other day, I was driving to my hairdresser and the people who were behind me were practically leaning on their horns. They honked and honked, and then they zoomed, they *zoomed* around me on my right hand side where I can't see because of that pinched nerve in my neck. I tell you the traffic was *merciless.*

(Pause)
No wonder I didn't see that ridiculous bus.

(Pause)
Whatever happened to common courtesy? People used to show you some respect. They used to wave you through intersections. They used to look before they merged. They used to blink their lights when the police were up ahead. Now, it's every man for himself.

(Pause while she re-arranges flowers)
Not to mention what it's like to go into a repair shop these days, if you can even find one. They speak a different language there. It's all about fuel injection systems and electronic dashboards. They have to look at their computers just to tell you you've got

7

a flat. And everything's gotten so expensive. Just a few bumps and scrapes and they charge you an arm and a leg.

(*Removes compact from purse, checks makeup*)
They charge you so much, you have to get the insurance company involved and then your daughter gets all superior with you.

(*Puts compact back in purse*)
And the *police*. Well, let me tell you, there was a day when a fine young police officer might take off his hat to you. He might offer you his arm and a kind word. But, today, all you get is a lecture. A nasty lecture. Like no else has ever forgotten all those papers that they tell you to keep in your car. Listen, Mr. Policeman, when I take all those prescription medicines, I'm lucky if I remember who I am and you want to know where I live?

(*Adjusts bandage*)
Oh, I remember where I live all right. I remember all too well.

(*Pause*)
I live with my, oh, so caring daughter and her, oh, so caring hubby and they have a swimming pool and three TVs and two damn cars.

(*Shakes finger*)
But they don't have any children.

(*Sarcastic gratitude*)
So thank you, Mr. Policeman. Thank you for driving me home after giving me a lecture about responsibility because, then, I have to get a lecture from my daughter, too.

(*Pause*)
She didn't even ask me whether I got hurt. She didn't ask me

about the bump I got on my head. She just wanted to complain about her missing headlight.

(*Angry*)
It's my fault, she says, it's always my fault.

(*Puts hand to her heart*)
Mea culpa, mea maxima culpa.

(*Snorts*)
Okay, little Miss Superior, I know I didn't exactly ask you whether I could take (*air quotes*) "your" car to go shopping, but so what? You owe me.

(*Pause*)
Who do you suppose drove you to all those ballet lessons and paid for them, too? I bet those lessons cost as much as *two* fenders would. Who drove you to get all those nice clothes you wore to school? You never worried about what sort of wear and tear I put on *my* car. All you cared about was getting to where you wanted to go. *You* didn't care how many headlights *I* had left when I got her there.

(*Throws hands in air*)
So take the keys away. You don't think I've got another set? You bet I do even if it cost me $200 to get them. You'd think they were made of plutonium or something.

(*She hoots*)
I know how you take that oh-so-wonderful *public transportation* to work every morning, so you can brag about saving the environment, leaving me at home, stuck in the middle of suburbia with nothing to do. Heck, you probably should thank me for taking your car out of operation and putting it in the shop. Just think of all the pollution I eliminated.

(*Pause*)

9

(*Pause*)

How do you think I'm going to spend my remaining years? Watch one of your TVs all day long? Maybe if you'd had some kids I'd have something to do around here, but you don't.

(*Disinterested*)
Anyway, didn't your insurance pay for most of the damage? Didn't you get your car back in just a few weeks? Doesn't it look all shiny and bright sitting there in your garage?

(*Pause*)
And do you think that I'm never going to use it again just because you told me not to?

(*Raises voice*)
Well, I'm going to go for a drive and you can't stop me. I'm going to get in that car and unless you've hidden the electronic opener again I'm going to raise that big old garage door and then back out into the street.

(*Pause*)
In that order - I've learned from my mistakes.

(*Raises voice*)
We'll see who's gotten too old and senile to drive. There's a mall with a Dollar Tree and a Ross about a mile down the road and if I take the highway I'll be there within a couple of hours.

(*Gleeful*)
And if anyone tries to get in my way, I don't care what happens or what it does to somebody's insurance rates. Mama gotta drive.

ANTS

Overhead lights come up over two men. The first man, Bernard, is in bright light. He is wearing normal business attire. The second, a man seated in a chair, is seen more dimly. Bernard is sitting before a console with a number of switches and dials. A single wire runs from the console to the man in the chair where it splits into several smaller wires each of which is attached to patches attached to the body of the man in the chair who has a burlap bag over his head.

BERNARD
Mysterious affair, electricity.

(Bernard flicks a switch at the console. The man in the chair screams.)
It stimulates, does it not?

(Pause while Bernard picks up a clipboard and looks over the papers clipped to it)
Perhaps you could help us with our inquiries about your friends. After all, your friends have already told us so much about you. It would only be reciprocal for you to tell us about them.

(Pause)
May I say you are lucky to have such friends? They were all quite complimentary about you. They all said you are da bomb. Don't worry. We will never make the tapes public.

(Bernard looks up from clipboard)
I'm sorry, I'm sure I didn't make myself clear. I'm looking for a response.

(Bernard flicks a switch at the console. The man in the chair screams.)
Isn't it funny about friends? Sometimes you really need to have someone around to talk to, but sometimes you think that it

would just make everything worse if you told anyone about the thing that is most important to you. I mean, it's only human to have secrets.

(Pause while Bernard looks through the papers on the clipboard)
Perhaps you often meet Delores down at the place we shall not mention. Perhaps you would be surprised to learn that Delores has been very cooperative with us. Perhaps you would be surprised to learn that Delores gets her decorating tips from us.

(Pause)
Don't worry. No one need ever know.

(Pause)
Do you like that phrase? We often use it at the station. We often talk about you at the station. We like the way you wear your hair, but we think that you should call your mother more often. I know she would appreciate hearing from you. Don't you think so?

(There is no response. Bernard throws the switch again. The man in the chair screams.)
Really, she's a saint.

(Pause)
Don't worry. We will burn the documents after we have read them.

(Bernard puts clipboard down)
Perhaps there is a favor you would like from us. Perhaps there is someone you would like to meet, someone powerful who could help you advance you in your career. I believe that you consider yourself artistic. We are very encouraging of artists of all ethnic backgrounds. Perhaps you could qualify for one of our very liberal grants. Don't worry. We will destroy the questionnaires once the information is entered into our data bank.

(Bernard throws the switch again. The man in the chair screams.)
Really, would it kill you to make a little conversation? I feel like I'm just talking to myself here.

(Bernard looks up at the ceiling. He seems to be talking to himself)
In these situations, there is always a question whether to apply the electro-shock. The physical condition of the subject must be considered as must the possibility of incurring any side effects which would render the procedure less than efficacious. There are often ethical questions as well, particularly in the matter of how consent may be given.

(Pause)
Don't worry. We will keep your responses confidential.

(Pause)
I can understand your feelings. That letter was a shock. What your friend told you was a shock. Her death was a shock.

(Impatient)
Do you remember any of these things? I would appreciate an answer.

(Bernard adjusts a dial on the console and flips the switch again. The man in the chair groans.)
It is possible for the electrical stimulant to block the reoccurrence of certain memories in the subject. It is also possible that the electrical stimulant will cause the subject to experience memories that have long been repressed.

(Pause)
Don't worry. We will not count the experimental section against your final score.

13

(Bernard throws the switch again, but the man in the chair does not respond)
Perhaps it would help us with our inquiries if you were to tell us your dreams. Dreams, after all, are a way into the soul. Dreams can be analyzed. Dreams can be tested. We have an entire section of specialists dedicated to dream interpretation. Once you share your dreams with us we will understand you better.

(Meditative)
Perhaps it would help if I were to tell you one of my own dreams. Then, perhaps, you will feel comfortable responding with a dream of your own and so a connection can be made and we will become friends.

(Stands up and paces while he talks)
I was standing in my garden drinking a cup of coffee (as I do most mornings) when I noticed a vine had twined itself through the boxwood hedge that surrounds my patio. I had never noticed it before although it, that is, the vine, had grown quite profusely twining itself around all the branches of the boxwood and now it was starting to break into bloom with purple and white flowers. They were quite attractive these flowers and so I reached over to break one of them off of its stem maybe to put it in a vase with water, but as soon as I had touched it an ant ran down the flower and onto my hand and that ant was followed by thousands of others. In a second they had run up my arm and down my clothing and had locked themselves onto my skin with their teeth, but instead of pain, what I felt was memories, thousands of them. Each ant was carrying a memory and each bite passed the agony of that memory to me. Some of the memories were trivial, but some were of the experience of death itself.

(Pause)
When I awoke I could not be sure whether I was truly awake or whether I was re-living one of the memories that I had received.

(Sits down)
Afterwards, I had my hedges sprayed to kill all the ants.

(Bernard throws the switch again. The man in the chair slumps to his side)
Throughout his writings Freud used the word, *"seele,"* which means "soul." However, in English this word has been translated as "mind."

(Pause)
If there were a soul, do you think it would be essentially electrical, or do you think it is more likely it would be chemical? It is important that you share your opinion on this matter.

(Impatient)
If the soul is electrical in nature, then a connection would be possible between the circuitry and the object to be acted upon. Furthermore, the direction of the flow would alternate between them. There would be transference and countertransference. Information would be exchanged freely between the two poles. Everything would be known.

(Pause)
But if the soul is chemical, well, good luck with that.

(Pause)
Coupled to another, the soul sparks and burns. Uncoupled, the soul becomes ... what?

(The light above the man in chair goes out. Bernard flips the switch. There is no response.)
You might as well answer me. Before we are through I will know your soul as thoroughly as I know my own.

(Bernard fiddles with the console, but the light does come on again)

Don't worry. We will get rid of the body. No one need ever know.

(The lights go down)

THE KAFKA PROCESS

The lights come upon Dr. Hermann, who is standing up and facing the audience when the lights come up. Behind him is the desk on which the printer is running. He stands to the side of the whiteboard. He addresses the audience as if he were speaking to someone well known to him. He is confident and cheerful in the manner of someone who has achieved a successful outcome in some important enterprise. Although he seems to be in a good mood, he appears to be somewhat perfunctory when he talks to Joseph, who is not seen on stage. At times, he appears to speaking only to himself.

DR. HERMANN

Good to see you again, Joseph. It's nice to have you on board today. You've arrived at the perfect time to help us finish what we all consider to be the most successful Kafka product yet. I know that you were very involved in our start-up. You'll find that we've made great progress since then.

(Moves to printer and picks up print out which he reads for a moment before looking up at audience)
Let me give you a rundown of the whole project.

(Moves to whiteboard)
Forgive me if I'm going over things that you already know, but it'll be easier for me to explain how the project has changed if I start at its beginning.

(Clears his throat as if beginning a prepared speech)
In order to create a new work of fiction by Kafka we begin by randomly selecting a sentence from his published stories. The one we used for the project that you're involved in was "For we are like tree trunks in the snow." We'll call this the "germ" of the story.

(Erases some of the figures on the whiteboard with an eraser, writes "G: tree trunks" on whiteboard)
To this sentence we added another also taken from Kafka's works. The second sentence that the computer randomly selected was "Often he lay there the long nights through without sleeping at all, scrabbling for hours on the leather."

(Writes "+ S2: long nights" on whiteboard and stands back looking at board of a moment before turning back to audience)
Of course, Kafka's statement concerning the trees could not normally be expected to generate a second statement involving a person who would "lay there the long nights through."

(Laughs)
However, the distinguishing feature of the Kafka process is the way our program toggles through the first two sentences and incorporates them through machine logic to create a new third sentence in Kafka's own style.

(Reads from print out while stroking his chin)
You see here that the program has created a passage that reads, "He was as insensible as a tree trunk in the snow as he lay there the long nights through."

(Continues talking with disinterest)
Now the process has chosen a third passage from Kafka. This is added to the mix, then, a fourth and a fifth, *und so weiter,* as Kafka himself might have said.

(Looks up from print out)
I know that you would have preferred that we work in German, but management decided that our audience, which is largely American, would prefer to have a product that was drafted in American rhythms and which employed American idiom.

(Puts print out down)

18

So, Joseph, when you were last working with us we were operating on the theory that, given sufficient time and computing power, this process would produce a work of literary fiction in Kafka's voice.

(Pause)
But what we found was that our Kafka product was essentially directionless. The prose did not proceed naturally towards a catharsis.

(Looks away from audience as though lost in his own thoughts)
Look at the wonderful irony in such works as "In the Penal Colony" and "The Trial." But our Kafka process, as it originally functioned, was unable to generate an ending that was aesthetically satisfying.

(Strokes chin)
We tried adding realistic elements taken from newspapers, such as murders and criminal trials and political scandals, to guide the computer, but, as you may recall, the material that we got back was only sensationalistic and not imaginative or insightful about the human condition. The process generated language that was recognizably Kafkaesque, but our story was lacking the human element.

(Pause)
After the top staff brain-stormed the problem, we determined that what was needed was a human model functioning in real-time. We, therefore, agreed to select an individual and to set him upon a path of tragedy.

(Looks back toward front of stage)
We only needed to track the individual's responses to the events to create a template, if you will, for an entirely new Kafka product.

(Pause)

19

And that is why we fired you and spread rumors that you had provided proprietary information to our competitors. Your subsequent alcoholism and paranoid delusions as well as your divorce and near death in a car accident were perfect material for a Kafka novel.

(Seems very pleased with himself)
I must say, the fact that you have now appeared at our facilities with a gun and have announced your determination to destroy the machinery that is even now producing the story of your life is such an appropriately Kafkaesque development that the whole experiment must be regarded as a great success.

(Reaches for printout)
Just a second, please, Joseph, I want to read you what, I must say, is a beautiful description of your impending suicide. I really don't think that Kafka could have done it any better.

HALF A LOAF

The lights come up on Victor sitting at the table. Victor appears to be in his thirties and has dark, messy, shoulder-length hair. He wears a VFW cap and a camouflage jacket with an empty left sleeve. He speaks with a rural accent. There is a mug and a pitcher of beer on the man's side of the wire. The man is looking downward when we first see him, but after a few moments, he faces the audience and takes a sip from the beer mug. His manner is that of someone telling a story for the hundredth time. He shows very little emotion while he speaks except for those times when he pretends to be one of the other characters.

VICTOR

After an IED blew off my arm, the angels seized it and took it to Heaven to await the ascension of the remainder of my body, which was expected to be coming in the near future.

(Pause)
Instead, I survived.

(Drinks from his mug)
After medical treatment I was given a discharge from the service and sent home to resume my normal, pre-war life. It was expected that I would find work at Goodwill, or, maybe, in a sheltered workshop. But I was not that same young man who had signed his enlistment papers in the hope of seeing something of the world. I started to drink and use drugs and get into arguments with anyone who tried to tell me what to do. And so I died long before I became an old man.

(Shrugs)
I appeared before the eternal court, but because of my sins I did not receive clearance to pass into Heaven and was, instead, sentenced to a term in Hell.

(Pause)

Although my body took up residence in Hell, my left arm continued to live in Heaven. I could visit my arm, but only at irregular intervals when a shuttle would transport me to a checkpoint at the border between Heaven and Hell. There, I sat on one side of a room that was divided by barbed wire. My arm rested on the other side of the wire although the fingers of my left hand were allowed to stroke the fingers of my right hand while I told my left arm about how things were going in Hell.

(Lifts his right arm and wraps his fingers around the barbed wire, sighs)
The only other person I saw at the checkpoint was a blind man who came to visit his eyes.

(Pause)
One day, as he was leaving to return to Heaven the blind man brushed against my left arm.

(Stands and puts his right hand across his eye and speaks in the voice of an old man)
Please excuse me sir, I was unaware that anyone else was here.

(Speaks again in his own voice)
That's not a man, just an arm. My arm's in Heaven and I'm in Hell.

(In the voice of an old man)
Ah, then we are in similar positions. My eyes have been sent to Hell because they are evil. Despite all the good things in the world, my eyes insisted on showing me only what was bad. Therefore, I plucked them out from their sockets and sent them off to have holy judgment imposed on them. Yet, I must admit that I miss them and that I have hoped to reconcile with them some day.

(In his own voice)

The blind man took the shuttle back to Heaven. The next time that he met with his case worker, the blind man asked if there was any chance that my left arm could be sent to me in Hell in exchange for his eyes which could be returned to him in Heaven. He said that it was a way for us both to be complete again.

(Small chuckle)
The caseworker passed the idea to his supervisor and the supervisor told his manager and so on up the chain of angel hierarchy from cherubim to archangel until God heard about and decided it might get him some good press.

(Takes another sip from his mug, walks around the corner of the desk to stand in front of the table)
So before long, an angel wearing an Italian linen suit and a tie that was the blue-green color of a mountain lake was in conference with an emissary of the Devil who was dressed in a black suit and a fiery red tie.

(Pause)
The angel spoke first, as angels always do.

(Speaks in the voice of a self-satisfied, somewhat patronizing lawyer)
Look, this can be a win-win situation. We give your side a little something and you give us a little something back. You know how these things work. Two people are made happy and the balance between Heaven and Hell is maintained.

(Speaks in his own voice)
The Devil's emissary was not so sure.

(Speaks in an edgy, irritated voice)
I don't know why you took that blind guy, anyway. I mean, he tore out his own eyes and then he couldn't work, so he impoverished his own family. If anything, he should be on our

side of the fence. Besides, aren't two good eyes more valuable than one left arm? I don't think you're offering us fair compensation here.

(Pause)
The negotiations went on for a while and then a bureaucratic solution was worked out that was like a lot of other bureaucratic solutions. The blind man was sent to Hell, where he thought that he would be re-united with his eyes, but that didn't happen because his eyes were taken to Heaven and given into the custody of my left arm.

(Shrugs)
No surprise. That's always how things work.

(Takes another drink, stands up, walks back and forth for a moment before he looks out at audience and speaks in a resigned voice)
So, now, I have the blind man as my housemate.

(Pause)
He's not bad company, though, even if I have to take care of the cooking and the cleaning for him, but I usually can leave him alone in the evenings and go out by myself. He's happy enough with the situation because I've lied to him. I've told him it's hot because the air conditioner is on the fritz and I've told him the wails of the damned are teenagers with boom boxes and that the demons that rub against his legs are just the neighborhood cats.

(Raises his voice and speaks with more intensity)
Meantime, from what I hear, my arm is upset with the new situation. Since it hooked up with the eyes, my arm now can see all of Heaven with its skyscrapers and its courts of law and its ranks of angels singing hymns of praise. But anything the eyes show him seems somehow less glorious than my arm expected.

(The man snorts and shakes his head)
A few days ago I met with my arm at the checkpoint.

(The man tries to speak with confidence, but his voice trails off into resignation)
I assured my arm that before long they'd get things straightened out and we'd be together again, even though we'll be in Hell. I told him that Hell was no different than any other place you might get stuck in.

(The man sits down and finishes his mug of beer)
I know I've been in places that were a lot worse.

(The man looks up at the audience)
And I said don't bring those creepy eyes with you when you come. They're just a pair of trouble makers and, anyway, there's nothing you'd really want to see down here. It's better just to make things up, if you really want to be happy.

Lights down.

25

THANK YOU

The lights come up on God in a white robe standing center stage and holding a microphone. He appears to be in his sixties or seventies and has a full, white beard.

GOD

(Enthusiastic)
Thank you, ladies and gentlemen. Thank you, thank you, for your applause. Thank you so much for your support and your enthusiasm. Let me say very sincerely, I couldn't do it without you, folks. I really couldn't. Thank you, thank you. Audiences like you are why I get up and do this every night.

(Musing)
... get up and do this every night.

(Puts hand to forehead)
And your card is the eight of diamonds. Am I correct? Hold up your card, sir, please, let everyone see it. Thank you, thank you, so much. Please, you're too good. Thank you.

(Waves)
Such a wonderful place, I always love coming here. Really, I give my best performances here, especially when I get an audience as great as this. Sincerely, you're the best.

(Motions with palms down to hush audience, contemplate)
The number you're thinking of, madam, is seventeen. Am I correct? No, no, I can't tell you how I do it. Not a trick, ladies and gentlemen, it's something I was just born with. It's a gift, really. Can't tell you how I do it. Thank you, thank you so much. No, really, you're too good. Here's where I feel it.

(Puts hand over his heart)
Lots of good feeling here, tonight, lots of good feeling. My dearest hope is that I can leave you a little happier than before.

(Musing)
... just take a little of your pain away.

(Looks toward audience)
Hold up your purse, madam. Yes, hold it out in front of you. That's right. Now concentrate on your purse. Thank you. I am getting an image of an address book. It has a paper cover and is brown in color. Inside the address book is an entry for a Ms. Elma Mayhew. She lives in Apartment 23 on Nightingale Court. Am I correct? Thank you, thank you. Thank you very much.

(Raises voice)
How am I doing folks? I hope that you like our little show. And I want to know how much I appreciate all the love you're sending out tonight. Just keep those cards and letters coming, right? Ha. Ha. I admit it, folks, I just can't get enough of your good wishes. Thank you, thank you, again.

(Looks toward audience)
Is there a Betty Barden out there? Betty Barden? Yes, please stand up, Ms. Barden. That's right. Let's get a light on Ms. Barden.

(Puts hand to forehead)
I'm getting a message for you, Ms. Barden. It's a message from the other side. It's from your brother, Ernie. He wants you to know that he's happy. He wants you to know that he is in no pain now. Also, he wants you to know that there is a suitcase, a brown leather suitcase, up in the attic of your house. It's next to the ceramic clock that your father left you. He says that inside the suitcase you will find a lottery ticket. And that lottery ticket is a winner. It's worth a thousand dollars, Ms. Barden. Yes, a thousand dollars. That's a very nice message isn't it? Wasn't that kind of your brother to let you in on that little secret?

(Quiets audience)

Thank you so much. I'm just glad I can be of help. Really, I like nothing better than to make things a little better for you all. That's all I want. Thank you, thank you.

(*Laughs*)
Now, Ms. Barden, I know you want to get home to find that suitcase. Honestly, I would, too, but just hold on a minute. The show is almost over.

(*Musing*)
... almost over.

(*Pause*)
Well, I guess you've heard that this is our closing night. It's been a great little run, hasn't it? I can't tell you how much I appreciate audiences like you and, really, you've been one of the best. Please, give yourself a hand. That's it, make some noise. You deserve it.

(*Stands with head bent while he accepts applause*)
There's always been such energy in this place. I confess I'll miss it. I'll miss coming out here every night and feeling the love you give me. And, I hope you know that I reciprocate and that I love you, too. But, you know how it is when you're a performer. You want to keep things fresh. There's always new material to try out.

(*Pause*)
And let me say once again, Earth has always been one of my favorite creations.

(*Musing*)
... been a good run.

(*Raises hand above head, shouts into microphone*)

29

And now, ladies and gentlemen, for our big finish. I trying something different here, so we'll just have to see how it goes. I hope I don't screw it up.

(*Chuckles*)
Nothing up my sleeve, folks. No mirrors, no smoke. Just pure magic.

(*Shouts dramatically*)
Let there be dark!

(*Lights go down*)

INSUFFICIENCY

A spotlight comes up on center stage. From the darkness, Paul, a man in his late fifties or early sixties, dressed in a white cotton shirt and black pants and seated in a wheelchair, wheels himself into the light. He adjusts his position and addresses the audience.

PAUL

There was a great famine in the country and the authorities had seized our crops.

(Pause)
They promised that they would make an equitable division of all the available food and return a fair share to us.

(Turns hands over)
After all, one town grew grain, another fruit, a third raised cattle, and so on. No town could live on only what it produced, so there had to be a system by which goods were transferred.

(Pause)
When we traded among ourselves, inequalities occurred. For example, one year, there was so much fruit that the orchard owners could not charge enough to make up their production costs. Another year, there was so little grain that the farmers could charge astronomical prices for their wheat. As a result, the central authorities decided to take all of our food and distribute it equally among us.

(Wry grin)
This was done for many years with few complaints. However, after several years of poor crops, there was not enough food to feed everyone.

(Sighs)

I know this is boring, but before long I will tell you about the disaster that followed and that will make everything more interesting.

(*Pause*)
In the third year of the crop failures, we completed the requisition forms, as always, and had them stamped with the necessary certifications and done up in the appropriate ribbons.

(*Shrugs*)
We delivered the paperwork to designated officials. We paid the fees. We made a power point presentation to the head of the department. We cultivated members of the party in power. We left gifts on their desks. We sent them letters of commendation. We pulled down the old statues of the old leaders and put up new statues of the new leaders. We changed the names of our streets and public squares to reflect the new reality.

(*Pause*)
And yet, when the food arrived, we could see that it was not enough to feed everyone.

(*Clears throat*)
Our protestations were overlooked. Our inquiries were ignored. The authorities refused to grant an audience to our delegates.

(*Looks over shoulder*)

But we still needed more food.

(*Pause*)
We were not fools. We recognized that there was nothing left for us to do but to accept our insufficiency and to make plans to deal with it. Our leaders met, but could not reach any agreement about how to proceed. We, therefore, elected new leaders, but with no better results than before.

(*Plays with wheel*)
We realized that excluding some of us from the food we had would allow others of us to make do. By how could that be decided? No one would volunteer to starve.

(*Pause*)
We could vote, but who would recognize the legitimacy of such a vote? Who would honor it? It would simply come down to a power struggle that would destroy us all.

(Pause)

There was no one of high such standing in the community that we would agree to give the authority to decide who would be given food and who would be denied it. None of us had the moral authority to make a decision of such weight and importance.

(*Frustrated, turns palms over*)
We were deadlocked.

(*Rolls eyes, puffs lips*)
We then asked the authorities to appoint a judge who would decide the matter for us.

(*Seems to recover his narrative voice*)
He visited us, heard our concerns, spoke with the counsel and made a decision.

(*Pause*)
We did not like his decision, but we had all agreed that we would accept the consequences of any decision that this man made. And we also agreed that what he proposed was an equitable solution to our problem of whom should be fed.

(*Musing*)

We had expected that some of us might be required to leave. That was how we saw it, that some would stay and others would have to make their way to some other place, but that was not how it turned out.

(*Pause*)
The judge had mandated a different solution to our problem. In our town, there was a bridge of wooden planks supported by two ropes. The bridge allowed us to pass over a ravine. The judge commanded that we remove the planks from the middle of the bridge. We would play a game of tug of war. We were assigned to one of two teams. Each team held an end of the bridge. As the tug of war progressed, those pulled toward the middle of the bridge would drop through the hole in the bridge and so the population would be reduced.

(*Looks toward ceiling*)
Unfortunately, our predisposition toward fairness worked against us. We had sought to create two teams of equal strength. Neither team could prevail entirely against the other. The two teams moved back and forth across the bridge like a saw across a log, as one team brought the other to the edge and the other redoubled its efforts to keep from being pulled over.

(*Pause*)
In time, each team began to lose members through the gap. The leaders of each team had placed their weakest pullers at the front of the rope, so the first to fall into the river were older people, then children, then women, with neither team able to finish off the other.

(*Coughs*)
I was one of the first to go, but as fate would have it, I fell into thick mud along the side of the river. As I lay there with my back broken I watched while many of those whose names I knew fell to their deaths.

(*Pause*)
At the end, there were only a few of the strongest left. For an hour there was almost no movement, but gradually one side began to be dragged toward the middle of the opening.

(*Spits*)
The judge could have ended the contest but he did not. Eventually, one side perished entirely. Perhaps a third of the town was left alive. And so the survivors went to the judge and asked, "Now how will you feed those of us who are left? We still need enough food to survive the winter."

(*Pause*)
The judge answered, "You have your rations here. There are more than enough bodies to keep you the rest of you alive." He laughed and the soldier took him away to another village.

(*Pause*)
That is how we survived the famine. I was lucky that the others chose to tend to my wounds rather than let me perish. But there is always a kinship among survivors.

(*Lights go down*)

www.ingramcontent.com/pod-product-compliance
Lightning Source LLC
LaVergne TN
LVHW021548080426
835509LV00019B/2913